Bobby Businessman

The Story of Four Pigs

by Robert D. Trette & Max Trette

DORRANCE
PUBLISHING CO
EST. 1920
PITTSBURGH, PENNSYLVANIA 15238

Dorrance Publishing Co
585 Alpha Drive
Pittsburgh, PA 15238
Visit our website at *www.dorrancebookstore.com*

ISBN: 979-8-89211-255-0
eISBN: 979-8-89211-753-1

This is book is dedicated to my mother and father,

Marylou and Bud Trette.

A True Story.

Bobby Businessman

The Story of Four Pigs

OAKDALE
JOINT UNION HIGH SCHOOL
SCHOOL BUS

It was Bobby's first year of high school at Oakdale High. A fifteen-year-old freshman. The day came to decide what classes to enroll in.

Bobby met with the school counselor. Together, they looked over a selection of classes. He saw a class titled Agriculture 101. This particular class was for future farmers. Bobby is a future farmer. He and his father were together many times at the family ranch. In the early years his dad milked cows while Bobby cleaned and swept out the barn. Bobby enjoyed the independent life of being a rancher. The smells, different temperatures, freedom, and challenges was what it felt like to be a rancher. This was a class Bobby had interest in.

Bobby joined the school club, **The Future Farmers of America,** the **FFA.** Becoming a future farmer also meant being initiated into a farming attitude. Bobby had an initiation by the older agriculture students. The new class of boys all lined up as the older class of agriculture students dipped both their hands into green paint. This green paint told their parents, friends, and the world they belonged to the **FFA.** The students were not allowed to wash the green paint off their hands for one week. Plenty of time to feel silly and *branded.*

First day of Agriculture class began. The teacher, Mr. Hutchinson, asked each student to describe the ranch/farm they had grown up on. The teacher wanted to understand the type of crops or animals each student's families had on their ranches and farms.

There were about twenty boy students in this classroom. No girls. All new students, whom Bobby did not know. They all took a minute to describe the type and size of ranch each of them had grown up on.

Bobby was anxious and a little nervous. He did not know any of the boys and had never spoken in front of a large group.

It was Bobby's turn to speak. Bobby described the three-hundred-acre ranch that had been part of his family since 1886. His family harvested almonds and peaches. The teacher was building confidence into his students. In farming or business, you need confidence. Bobby found out he enjoyed speaking to a group. The experience of standing up and speaking felt like leadership. Bobby began to feel ranch ownership, which was what this class was really about.

In the first couple of weeks his teacher spoke about how to take care of your crops. Everything from how to prune a tree to irrigating the crop. This teacher had Bobby's full attention. Bobby looked forward to his Agriculture 101 class. The students were asked by the teacher to come up with a ranch project where each student would manage their farm.

Every agriculture student was now a member of the FFA and needed a ranching responsibility. Bobby had zero ideas for a ranch project. The teacher began to talk about ranching, farming, and the idea of making money. Making money! Bobby had not planned on making any money. He had never seen or heard anyone talk about making money.

Ranching felt like an endeavor, a not-for-much-profit operation. Making money at the ranch was in short supply. Bobby had never heard one adult discuss ranching and money in the same sentence. Mr. Hutchinson came to Bobby's desk and asked about ideas for his FFA project. He asked if there was a corral or pen at the ranch. Bobby said yes. The teacher suggested only one thing for Bobby that morning: "How about raising pigs? Once the pig is fully grown, you can sell it."

Bobby really liked the idea of selling and making money.

BANK
OF
ALIFORNIA

Making money became a real feeling and thought.

He wanted and needed independence. It was about then Bobby figured out independence cost money. To be independent and on your own is not free.

The first challenge for each student was that their parents had no money for an agriculture project. Immediately, he felt a roadblock to this new idea. The teacher told Bobby, "You will need two hundred dollars in cash! That two hundred will get you four small pigs."

Bobby's parents did not have two hundred dollars for a farming enterprise. Bobby is a poor farmer just like the rest of the class. First lesson, figure it out! Keep moving forward, but figure it out. Bobby learned that a worthwhile endeavor comes with challenges and problems. This new obstacle was about money.

Bobby went home, and his mother suggested talking with banker Bill Boston, the manager at the Bank of California, in downtown Riverbank.

MANAGER

"Maybe Bill will loan you the two hundred dollars." Bobby would never have thought about borrowing money from the local bank. He began to consider ways to overcome new obstacles.

Bobby had a small savings account at the Bank of California. Bill Boston was aware of Bobby's long family history in the small community of Riverbank, CA. Bobby jumped onto his red bicycle and then walked into the bank. Bill was dressed for success. He waved Bobby over. Bobby explained to Bill the idea of wanting to borrow two hundred dollars for his FFA pig project. Bill listened to Bobby's idea and then asked questions. The loan was approved, and Bobby signed a loan document promising to pay back the two hundred dollars plus interest upon the sale of his four pigs.

Bobby was learning how to earn independence and respect. Shaking hands, speaking clearly with eye contact. Bobby was being trusted. This project was his responsibility.

RIVERBANK HOG FARM
FORD
HRH

His parents were not involved except to suggest the course of action. Bobby had to have the ability to raise pigs and pay off *his* loan. He felt responsible, and those feelings felt good. Bobby was excited, proud, trusted, and now in charge of his future.

Bobby had never held two hundred dollars. It was real exciting.

The next day Bobby and his teacher visited the hog farm. Bobby purchased four little pigs and put them in the back of his father's truck. They headed to the ranch. The ranch had a pig pen area that held the four little pigs. First year of high school and Bobby had four pigs to raise and fatten up. Responsibility toward the class, teacher, the banker, and his family, he felt positive.

Bobby began to learn many things from raising four pigs. First and foremost, pigs will eat just about anything. He quickly learned pigs have personalities. Pigs can smile. Pigs start off small but turn into big fat hogs. A good farmer loves his endeavor, his crop, and in his case, those four pigs.

Each night, after dinner, he and his father would take the daily scraps from the dinner table and feed the pigs. Pigs are smart. Once they figured Bobby was headed their direction with food and water, they became very excited. Pigs are pigs, they eat and eat.

A big challenge became finding enough food for these four pigs. He had never seen so much food eaten in such a short amount of time. Bobby was starting to realize more food was needed. Fattening up these animals was a big goal. A commitment towards the pig's healthy growth was made.

Bobby asked his father if he had any ideas about finding more food. They asked Bobby's Uncle Elmer, who lived in the ranch house, to bring food scraps from their home.

Bobby's dad worked at a company in Modesto, Milk Producers. Bobby's father would bring home spoiled milk products. This was just enough to keep fattening up these four pigs.

When Bobby purchased these four pigs they each weighed about fifty pounds. As the months went by the four pigs began to grow and grow, quickly becoming hogs. Walking around the pig pen became a challenge. Bobby was cautious not to get run over by fast-growing big hogs.

They grew and grew and grew. At some point Bobby had to kind of sneak up on them in order to place the food and water inside the pig pen. It was surprising how smart they were.

As he watched these hogs grow Bobby started to think if he could actually earn money. It was just a school project. Bobby was focused on taking good care of those four pigs. They ended up weighing four hundred pounds. Bobby began to think about selling his four hogs. Saying goodbye to his FFA project and four hogs.

Bobby and his dad made their end-of-day visit to the ranch. They discovered these four hogs were not very excited or happy to see them. They looked into the pig pen and noticed one of the hogs lying on the ground.

He was dead! The other hogs were acting strange. The three hogs were not smiling, and neither was Bobby or his father. Bobby could not believe that his FFA pig project had a real crisis. This was to become a personal farming problem. Bobby's problem to figure out. He asked Cousin David if he knew anything about the dead hog. Cousin David said, "A few of our friends came to the ranch and were teasing and riding the big hogs."

They buried hog number four at the ranch. Trust changed. It seemed everything changed. Bobby's attitude and the pig's attitude. The atmosphere went from positive to negative. Trust violated. Jealous friends are not friends.

Potential profit-making just decreased. Bobby's financial worth was now smaller. After being upset about the loss of one hog, Bobby had to get busy selling the remaining three hogs. Bobby owed the Bank of California over two hundred dollars. He would never let banker Bill down.

Reputation, respect, and trust were being earned. The lesson of being responsible to others and yourself was being self-taught. Setbacks in life happen. Always be prepared for disappointment and challenges. Bobby began to learn failure is all part of moving forward.

One of the valuable lessons Bobby learned about being a responsible farmer is the people who are around you. Choose your friends and associates wisely. Bobby picked a new circle of friendships.

Bobby has a trusting attitude. Bobby was trusting the sale of his three hogs would pay the bank debt to Bill Boston. The more you trust, the more you are trusted. Trusting people is one of life's big lessons. Trust until you cannot. Bobby enjoyed earning trust.

The last week of Bobby's Ag 101 class was about showing and explaining how each student's project did. Grades were issued on results. Bobby earned his first A+. He also earned a nice profit.

Bobby made a profit because he kept the cost of raising his pigs low. He ran down to the Bank of California and handed Bill Boston the money owed. Firmly shaking Bill's hand and thanking him for trusting a fifteen-year-old kid. Bobby explained to Bill that his potential profit was minimized by the loss of one pig. Bobby wanted Bill and the bank to have confidence in him. Entrepreneurial instincts told Bobby this was not his last loan with Bill Boston.

Bobby was farming trust…

Over ten years passed, and Bobby visited Bill Boston at the bank one last time. Bill welcomed Bobby with a big smile and firm hand-shake. Bobby learned how important it is to express gratitude. Bobby thanked Bill again for that first business loan, as they shook hands.

Bobby ended up meeting a pretty girl at Oakdale High School, got married, and started his big journey as an entrepreneur.

Bobby's Big Lessons

Listen.

Pay Attention to Life.

Setbacks mean setups.

Choices. Choose wisely.

Failure = Success

Write down your goals.

The future is happening today.

Be helpful to those around you.

Have passion.

As Walt Disney said, *"The more you are in a state of gratitude, the more you will attract things to be grateful for."*

A wish is only a wish until it becomes a goal

THE BEGINNING

Bobby's actual ranch.

Bobby's actual FFA class.